Shoes Last Longer in LA

Poems by Matt Schatz

Kung Fu Treachery Press

Rancho Cucamonga, CA

Copyright © Matt Schatz, 2024

First Edition: 1 3 5 7 9 10 8 6 4 2

ISBN: 978-1-958182-88-8

LCCN: 2024945831

Cover and title page images: Matt Schatz

Author photo: Jenna Hymes

Acknowledgments

The author wishes to acknowledge writer Brandi Carie's work in helping to edit, order and compile this collection. He also wishes to thank poet John Dorsey for his support and advice. Some of these poems originally appeared in *Light* as "Poems of the Week," and "Billy Collins and Lily Collins" was published in the magazine's Winter/Spring 2024 Issue. Other poems in this collection were posted on the author's social media pages, where his mother, Marilyn Schatz, was often the first to click "like."

Table of Contents:

ONE

Shoes Last Longer in LA / 1

Seasonal Affection Disorder / 2

The Dramaturg / 3

Eagle Rock Boulevard Haiku / 4

I Owe My Soul to the Village Bakery / 5

Hollywood Haiku #2 / 6

Atwater Village Thrift Store Find / 7

Baja Fresh Haiku / 8

California Roll / 9

Only Plums in the Icebox / 10

A Sonnet for Darryl Dawkins (1957 – 2015) / 11

My Father-in-Law / 12

Reverse Psychopathy / 13

Glendale Girl / 14

Sometimes Rhymezone.com Isn't Helpful / 15

Ancestry / 16

Practice / 17

Other Dads at the Annual Hanukkah Fair... / 18

Potential Memoir Title / 19

TWO

Folk Tales / 23

Uber Mensch / 24

Late Punctuation / 25

Larry Eisenberg (1919 – 2018) / 26

Admission Requirements / 27

Hollywood Haiku #1 / 28

Eagle Rock Coffee Shop Poem / 29

Excuse Me for Rhyming / 30

Scrapping a Song You've Written / 31

Executioner / 32

Deadline Article / 33

2020 or, This Isn't a Popularity Contest
    (or is it?) / 34

Malta Discovered / 35

A Kitchen Island of the Mind / 36

If I Were One of the Real Housewives
    This Would Be My Catchphrase / 37

Back Scratcher Haiku / 38

Love is Blind / 39

Radio Show Caller Haiku / 40

Fly-Ku / 41

Diagnosis / 42

Pandemic Diet / 43

I'm Not Positive but I Think it was Newton / 44

Harriet (My First Parenting Poem) / 45

Horology / 46

Billy Collins and Lily Collins / 47

THREE

Century City, Lightyears Away / 51

Cartoons / 52

Dear Dad / 53

Lyric Revision #1 / 54

William Goldman (1931 - 2018) / 55

Ballad of a Man with Children / 56

Haikea / 57

Adventures in the Stream Trade / 58

Personal Statement / 59

I Have Successful Artist Friends and / 60

Bridge / B Section for "The Itsy
   Bitsy Spider" Song / 61

I'm a Better Songwriter Than You Are / 62

Contract Negotiations / 63

Labor Intensive / 64

Another Heat Wave in the Birthplace
   of Panda Express / 65

WGA / 66

A Man Named Joyce / 67

Giving Tuesday / 68

Strike-Ku / 69

The New World Warbler or
   The Ways We Cope / 70

Old Pants / 71

It Actually May Be a Sentence / 72

Space-time, Sock-feet / 73

A Life in the Theater, or... / 74

FOUR

A Hurricane in Los Angeles / 77

Jewish Thanksgiving / 78

Housing Crisis / 79

For My Friend Angelique Govy (1981 – 2023) / 80

Exodus, or... / 81

This Poem Only Got One Like
   and It Was From My Mom / 82

War / 83

Location, Location, Location / 84

Song from 1995 / 85

Semitism / 86

Red-eye / 87

Killing Time at Grand Central While
 in Town for Two Play Readings
 and My Grandmother's Funeral / 88

The Upper West Side / 89

Haiku for the Jew / 90

At the Bookyard in Cherry Hill / 91

Regional Theater Pro Tip / 92

To the Tune of "Beauty and the Beast" / 93

Timothée Chalamet / 94

Bradley Cooper as Leonard Bernstein / 95

Helen Mirren and Bradley Cooper / 96

Semitism 2 / 97

The Shofar / 98

Miscommunication / 99

John Fitzgerald Kennedy Pitock (1962 – 2000) / 100

Alexander Graham Bell / 102

Our Parents Only Talk About the Past / 103

FIVE

New York City Scheming on Such
 a Summer's Night / 107

Airport Attire Haiku / 108

The Sandwich Island / 109

Schmuck Soup / 110

When I Get My Haircut / 111

Religious Observance / 112

Shane MacGowan (1957 – 2023) / 113

The Bees Knees / 114

Matt and Jenna and Ginsberg and Stegner / 115

The Dramatist / 116

Curriculum Vitae / 117

Old Books Smell So Sweet / 118

Jewish Optimism / 119

The Sixteen Million Greatest Living Jews / 120

Year in Review / 121

For Harriet on Her 4th Birthday / 122

For Jenna, Harriet and Millie

Not if it rhymes.

-Rodney Crowell
  when asked:
  "Are there things you withhold?"

One

Shoes Last Longer in LA

Shoes are stronger in LA
In New York, each sole is weaker
Shoes last longer in LA
Things are bleaker close to Bleecker
I'm a loafer in LA
In New York, I was a sneaker

Seasonal Affection Disorder

I love winter unconditionally
I love summer air-conditionally

The Dramaturg

Her theater has hoards
Of awards
She never gives notes
She gives chords

Eagle Rock Boulevard Haiku

I let a bus in
And the driver waved at me
I'm such a great guy

I Owe My Soul to the Village Bakery

You wrote 16 Puns
And what do you get?

Hollywood Haiku #2

You shouldn't trespass
Over at Henry Winkler's
No dogs, but sprinklers

Atwater Village Thrift Store Find

You've never been read
Slight dust jacket wear
One-dollar acquisition
And it has to be said
That I don't really care
You're the Book Club Edition

Baja Fresh Haiku

The guy in my line
Thinks he is better than me
He declined free chips

California Roll

Imitation crab
Is the sincerest form
Of flattery crab

Only Plums in the Icebox

I've heard that people
Have gotten sick
And have even died
From eating leftover fried rice
So I made sure to finish
The whole container
It wasn't easy
But safety first

A Sonnet for Darryl Dawkins (1957-2015)

On Planet Lovetron, he was born (he claimed)
But it made sense that he'd come from above
My fav'rite dunk (of all the ones he named)
Was one he called "The Walk Away From Love"

He broke a backboard once against the Kings
And later cracked another one (for luck)
When Stevie Wonder saw (or heard) such things
He dubbed him "Chocolate Thunder" (and it stuck)

To dream of him is to recall such sights
The shattered glass, the long and lovely limbs
He changed the game if just for those two nights
He changed the way the NBA made rims

But Planet Earth cannot contain such men
And so to Planet Lovetron, back again

My Father-in-Law

He called my poem Ogden Nashian
I wish such things were still in fashian

Reverse Psychopathy

While there may be exceptions
For certain isolated cases
There's a parking spot in Hell reserved
For those who back into spaces

Glendale Girl

Armenian Madonna
Auto-tuned soprano
Hot Americana
Iced Americano

Sometimes Rhymezone.com Isn't Helpful

Water boils, water freezes,
Water vaporizes.
Reprises sometimes rhymes with Jesus,
And other times with guises.

Ancestry

I'm an Amish composer
No buttons, just hooks

Practice

One perfect poem
In a lifetime of writing
Is a lot to ask

Other Dads at the Annual Hanukkah Fair at Silverlake Independent Jewish Community Center

Many a guy,
Bearded, portly,
Short of stature.
They nod "hi,"
Almost courtly...
Right back atcher!

Potential Memoir Title

I couldn't find a parking spot
So I just drove home

Two

Folk Tales

Hansel Culture
Gretel Culture
Cancel Culture
Shtetl Culture

Uber Mensch

I was hungry so I decided to get lunch first
But I'd already discussed with the driver
The fact that I was going to the library
So when he dropped me off
I walked towards the building
And up the front steps
Pausing and waiting until he'd pulled away
And was out of sight
Before crossing the street
I was a teenager in a movie
Embarrassed to reveal
To the parents of his new rich friend
Where his family actually lives

Late Punctuation

Rest in peace, sweet period
Your usefulness, once myriad
Was eroded by I.M. and text
With the point now in a casket
It's impossible to ask it
Which mark will leave us next?

Larry Eisenberg (1919-2018)

(Comment on his New York Times Obituary)

Larry Eisenberg, who for the Times

Wrote all of his comments in rhymes

Took news that was frightful

And made it delightful

And now up to heaven, he climbs

Admission Requirements

When you get to the gates of the afterlife
They don't ask, "How much did you give?"
The question is, "Did you ever drive fast
On a street where small children live?"

Hollywood Haiku #1

We just heard gunshots
They're shooting a crime drama
Two blocks from our house

Eagle Rock Coffee Shop Poem

One of the Gummers buys a latte
A guy from Girls plays chess
I work on a screenplay
Outside, the world's a mess

Excuse Me for Rhyming

When the photograph came
Painters' subjects blurred
But what in God's name
Occurred with the word?

Scrapping a Song You've Written

Decomposing

Executioner

The word you're looking for is executer

Deadline Article

'Year' Cancelled After Four Seasons.

2020 or,
This isn't a Popularity Contest (or is it?)

Dear students and citizens alike
It's a scientific fact
That Democracy and Covid spike
When people interact
But for the health of your fathers and mothers
We ask that you sequester
And that the Electoral College, like so many others
Be closed for at least this semester

Malta Discovered

(House Hunters International: Season 114, Episode 5)

This couple's search
For a prime place to perch
With the perfect Maltese balcony
Has a thrilling progression
From mere hunt to obsession
It's all very Maltese Falcony

A Kitchen Island of the Mind

When so often
I hear, "Forever Home"
I think of a coffin
Or a catacomb

If I Were One of the Real Housewives
This Would Be My Catchphrase

I used to be pensive
Now I'm ex-pensive

Back Scratcher Haiku

Tools were invented
'Cause we can't reach our whole backs
See also: Marriage

Love is Blind
(Reality Show)

When we were behind walls
We didn't put up facades
You're just not the person
I fell for in the pods

Radio Show Caller Haiku

Whatever they say
However great their question
I feel embarrassed

Fly-Ku

This fly in the house
It's all I can think about
It's like I'm in love

Diagnosis

I say I'm always anxious
But that's a disservice
I'm not always anxious
Sometimes I'm nervous

Pandemic Diet

A whole bowl full of solar eclipses
And a pocketful of apocryphal apocalypses

I'm Not Positive but I Think It Was Newton

I stand on the shoulders of giants
So said a great man of science
I'm glad he didn't live to see
The giants cut off at the knee

Harriet

(My First Parenting Poem)

I'll wash her bottle
If you'll change her diaper
We both changed her swaddle
So who's gonna wipe 'er?

Horology

I have an automatic German Bauhaus dress watch but
    don't move enough for the self-winding mechanism to
    self-wind
I have a gold-plated Hamilton watch from the 1970s that
    once belonged to my step-grandfather that I wore at my
    wedding nearly a decade ago now
I have another Hamilton mechanical field watch that I wear
    to take walks
I have a reasonably nice Timex that I packed away to mail
    to my father, but I've not made it to a post office
I have a ten-buck Casio digital that I was wearing the first
    time I held my daughter
And now she plays with whatever watch is on my wrist
Her tiny fingers touch the texture of the stainless steel
    bracelets
Drool pools on and stains the leather bands
And I'm careful when I pick her up not to poke her head
    with buckles and clasps
And I don't wear any watch at all to change her diaper
Not because I am protecting the watch, but because I am
    protecting her little butt
And time doesn't even really matter anymore anyway
The days go so slowly
The weeks go so fast
People say this is the worst year ever
I know what they mean of course
But every year is the worst and every year is also the best
Does that make sense?
I also have two Swatches

Billy Collins and Lily Collins

(Apologies to Robert Frost, my wife and everyone involved)

Some say your night should end with Billy,
Some say with Lil.
When winter weather's getting chilly
You could burn the books of Billy.
But if the night were colder still
I think I know enough of heat
To say that for conduction Lil
Could compete
And would fulfill.

Three

Century City, Lightyears Away

On the Avenue of the Stars
All the light that appears
Emanates from fancy cars
That have been broken down for years

Cartoons

We sat around on Saturdays
And satirized the sadder days

Dear Dad

Who has the best chin?
That is the question
Mine is hairy
Yours is cleft
But I always feared
If I shaved my beard
I'd have nary
A trace of chin left

Lyric Revision #1

(with apologies to Mack Gordon)

You make me feel so ~~young~~ old
You make me feel there are songs to be ~~sung~~ sold
Bells to be ~~rung~~ tolled
And a ~~wonderful fling to be flung~~ terrible thing to behold

William Goldman (1931-2018)

Old man, Goldman
The screenplays you sold, man
The stories you told, man
Gold, man

Ballad of a Man with Children

Your store doesn't open until eleven?
I could have sworn I read ten.
I had my breakfast at seven.
And I'd been up two hours by then.
A sensible time might be... nine?
I could make a great case for eight.
Split the difference? Eight-thirty? Fine!
But eleven? That's far too late!

Haikea

You get to the end
There is no frozen yogurt
What's the FJANTIG point?

Adventures in the Stream Trade

Baseball's got pitches
Basketball, passes
Screenwriters see things
Through half-empty glasses
Still, we wake up each day
And we pray they are takers
We make like the Dodgers
They make like the Lakers

Personal Statement

All I do are dishes
All I eat are fishes
All I make are wishes

I Have Successful Artist Friends and

My bitterness
Is hit or miss

Bridge / B Section for
"The Itsy Bitsy Spider" Song

See, the Itsy Bitsy Spider
He wanted to be a writer
But his talents did not that way tend
Once, years ago, he acted
As "Background Arachnid"
In a short film directed by his grad school friend
But he didn't have the legs
And now he's with the dregs

So, the Itsy Bitsy Spider
Went up the water spout...

I'm a Better Songwriter Than You Are

You may be a virtuoso
But the songs you write are so-so
Take your fingers off that fiddle
Try to fucking live a little

Contract Negotiations

Getting paid by the word?
Absurd
Make each syllable
Billable

Labor Intensive

Standing up for what is right
Sitting up awake at night
Walking when it's hot and sunny
Running quickly out of money

Another Heat Wave in the Birthplace of Panda Express

I have burned
And returned
Many a caloria
At the Glendale Galleria

WGA

To be a writer is stupidity
To be a writer is disparity
To be a writer, no liquidity
To be a writer, solidarity!

A Man Named Joyce

I think AI could never be
A TV writer good as me.

A guy who says, "I'm so deprest"
While dripping eel sauce on his chest;

A scribe who stares at screens all day,
And lifts his arms and screams, "Oy vey;"

A man that may in winter wear
That viral sweater from "The Bear;"

Something something writer's block;
Who rents a place in Eagle Rock.

Scripts are made by fools like me,
AI can 3D print a tree.

Giving Tuesday

So many theaters wrote me today
But it wasn't to tell me they're doing my play

Strike-Ku

If this thing goes on
You'll have to sell the Prius
To feed your fam'ly

The New World Warbler or The Ways We Cope

When I feel anxiety
I do word association
Audubon Society
Is a bird association

Old Pants

This Hanukkah we're low on gelt,
And I'm no friend to moneylenders.
I thought of tightening my belt.
Instead, I asked for new suspenders.

It Actually May Be a Sentence

He remembers then
And way back when
And still, he's undeterred
Age, he says, is not a number
It's a motherfucking word

Space-time, Sock-feet

I return to the past nightly
But I'm afraid of making sounds
So I tread oh so lightly
On my one-time stomping grounds

A Life in the Theater,
or I Once Sold Snickerdoodles in the Lobby
of Philadelphia's Arden Theatre Company

You start out selling concessions
You end up making them

Four

A Hurricane in Los Angeles

If all the tall palm trees
Finally break
And fall into the boulevard
Which now is a lake
We will know so called "car culture"
Was a mistake

Jewish Thanksgiving

Misgivings

Housing Crisis

Put the gentrification font
On a gentrification fence
And hackles are raised
As well as rents

For My Friend Angelique Govy (1981-2023)

I can't even
But I can odd

Exodus

or a response in light verse to two consecutive articles in
the Philadelphia Inquirer concerning the announcement
of the Geffen Playhouse's production of my musical A
Wicked Soul in Cherry Hill. The first from February 9,
2022, whose headline read, "A Cherry Hill rabbi hired a
hitman to murder his wife. Now, there's a musical about
the case. Sub-headline: "A new musical by Matt Schatz,
who grew up in South Jersey, explores the impact of
the 1994 murder of Carol Neulander, whose husband
is serving a life sentence for arranging to have her
killed." And the second on February 11, 2022, whose
headline read: "Carol Neulander's family 'saddened and
dismayed' by new musical 'A Wicked Soul in Cherry
Hill,' with the sub-headline: "The three children of
Carol Neulander, who was murdered by a hitman her
husband, a rabbi, hired, are outraged by a planned
musical theater piece about the 1994 Cherry Hill crime
and its aftermath." OK, now here's the poem:

This isn't exactly news
But unless you're Leon Uris
Writing about the Jews
Is hardly worth the tsuris

This Poem Only Got One Like and It Was from My Mom

Great work will spark a renaissance
And mine elicits no response
I focus only on the latter
And that, my dear is what's the matter

War

We fight about what drives more traffic
Graphic info or an infographic

Location, Location, Location

I never claimed to be
A Hist'ry PhD
And I'm no Nostradamus
And yet I understand
That ev'ry promised land
Will someday break its promise

Song from 1995

I try to spell your melody
I write down, "m.e.l.o.d…"
But before I get to "y"
I sit down on the ground and cry

Semitism

I have a little dreidel
I made it out of metal
I'll use it as a weapon
When the Cossacks storm the shtetl

Red-eye

I'll sleep
You think
Not a chance
Not a wink

Killing Time at Grand Central While in Town
for Two Play Readings and My Grandmother's
Funeral

Where Posman Books once was
There will be a Warby Parker
New York needs glasses because
The outlook is getting darker

The Upper West Side
First Date, 1962
This is a Haiku

Not much in common
But they both loved "All My Sons"
He meant, "My Three Sons"

Haiku for the Jew

Lox-eating boomers
Who refuse to try sushi
I just don't get it

At the Bookyard in Cherry Hill

I saw a book by a Heather O'Brien
I went to school with a Heather O'Brien
It isn't the same Heather O'Brien
But whatever happened to Heather O'Brien?

Regional Theater Pro Tip

If your play's not reducible
To a fun signature drink
It's not unproducible
But you'd be wise to think
Before you waste your ink

To the Tune of "Beauty and the Beast"

Never a surprise
Not exactly news
Tale as old as time
Song as old as rhyme
People hate the Jews

Timothée Chalamet

He's just like Gene Wilder but lit'ler
Only in theaters, this Holliday Season
Roald Dahl once said that Hitler,
"...didn't pick on the Jews for no reason."

Bradley Cooper as Leonard Bernstein

Look, I'm no critic
But if your nose is prosthetic
It may be antisemitic
Or else it's antisemetic

Helen Mirren and Bradley Cooper

First Lenny, my nose!
Now Golda, my ear!
Hath not a Jew eyes?
Nor an acting career?

Semitism 2

I have a little dreidel
I made it out of water
I scoop it with a ladle
And make soup for my daughter

The Shofar

Tonight's the Jewish New Year
And I'm a Jewish poet
We don't ring in the New Year
We close our eyes and blow it

Miscommunication

I asked you for the antidote
You told a poignant anecdote
I said, "That's great! My only note:
There's poison dripping down my throat."

John Fitzgerald Kennedy Pitock (1962-2000)

Was born Chu-Young Kim and was adopted by my mom's
    parents when he was four
And by the time I got to know him he was already a
    disappointment

His room was dark and cramped and it smelled from what
    I'd later learn was pot
And he played Kiss solos on a black and white Gibson
    Explorer

And one time when I was twelve he let me and my friend
    Ranaan hold his gun
And Ranaan later said to me your Uncle Johnny is so cool

How old do you think he is I asked and Ranaan guessed
    sixteen
I didn't have the heart to tell him that Uncle Johnny was
    almost thirty

I inherited the guitar and I smell that room whenever I
    open the hardshell case
The plush velvet interior has locked in its fibers a portal
    to the past

Odor molecules can last longer than those responsible
    for them
I never could play solos and I never got into Kiss

The guitar doesn't really suit me
It's heavy and awkward and the neck is thick for my
   small hands

But heirlooms have a way of adapting to their owners
Or maybe it's the other way around

So, I've come to love it
And it's come to love me

I have no idea what happened to the gun

Alexander Graham Bell

If my mom had invented the telephone
"Hello?" would become, "What's the matter?"
And if someone named Glass
Had invented the thing
Would it still ring?
Or shatter?

Our Parents Only Talk About the Past

We've heard all the stories before
But still, we listen
They are the opposite of fish stories
Because each time
The fish get smaller
And smaller
And we start to dread the day
Where they will
Disappear altogether

Five

New York City Scheming on Such a Summer's Night

I don't wanna live in LA no more
I don't wanna drive no car
I wanna go down to the drama bookstore
And I wanna see Here We Are
I wanna walk down a Brooklyn street
With my finger through the hole of a bagel
So I went to the crossroads
With my soul in a sack and said:
'This something that you can finagle?

Airport Attire Haiku

He is wearing shorts
At JFK in autumn
I am judgmental

The Sandwich Island

Bacon ham or sausage
Or you can get one without pork
No one makes an egg and cheese
Like New York

Eat it with your hands
Or use a plastic knife and fork
No one makes an egg and cheese
Like New York

Lots of spots to eat and drink
And even more to copy keys
But nothing makes New York, I think
Like an egg and cheese

Schmuck Soup

Zeppo, baby
Was a nepo baby
His father was Karl Marx
He learned about Communist Comedy
In the Lower East Side parks

When I Get My Haircut

At Fantastic Sam's
I hold my glasses
Beneath the black Barber's Cape
And I see my dad
Staring back at me
Except now he's bearded
And balding
And he is so goddamned handsome

Religious Observance

God, it turns out
Is a hater
Of the term
"Content creator"

Shane MacGowan (1957-2023)

In this beautiful world
There is terrible grief
The most beautiful singer
Had terrible teef

The Bees Knees

There are days not so sunny
Where I stare at my feet
And dig my toes into the soil
When I call you "my honey"
It's not 'cause you're sweet
It's because you never spoil

Matt and Jenna and Ginsberg and Stegner

Husband misreads poetry
Wife misreads prose
"angleheaded hipsters..."
"Angel of Repose"

The Dramatist

She felt like a fraud
'Cause she made it all up
Would they even applaud?
But they ate it all up
And she was so awed
When after the show
There was only one question:
How did you know?

Curriculum Vitae

My ambition used to be so big,
And now it's slightly less so.
I once said "Yes!" to every gig,
And now I say, "I guess so."

Old Books Smell So Sweet

I open you up
Nose to the page
Most other things
Sour with age

Jewish Optimism

The pickle is
Half sour

The Sixteen Million Greatest Living Jews

I usually hate these kinds of lists
But I clicked the link all the same
I scrolled and scrolled for weeks and weeks
And finally found my name

Year in Review

I wrote two plays
We had a second child
Domesticated days
My hair grew wild

For Harriet on Her 4th Birthday

Because some phrases fill us with sorrow,
There are new ones that we make up.
She's always hated the word "tomorrow;"
She calls it: "Later, when we wake up."

Matt Schatz is a writer and composer known for his plays and musicals *The Burdens, A Wicked Soul in Cherry Hill, An Untitled New Play by Justin Timberlake, The Past, A Present Yet to Come,* and many others. His work has been produced nationwide at theaters large and small and is published by Broadway Licensing and TRW Plays. Matt wrote the songs for Season 3 of the Spotify/Gimlet podcast series *The Two Princes.* He has had television and film projects sold to and developed for multiple studios and networks and has been in writers' rooms for AMC, Sony, and Netflix shows. He was a writer for Netflix Animation's *Charlie and the Chocolate Factory* adaptation, for which he also co-wrote the pilot with Oscar-winner Taika Waititi. Matt is currently co-writing a pilot for AMC and a new musical adaptation of *The Time Machine.* Awards include the Kleban Prize in Musical Theatre, the Reva Shiner Comedy Award, The ASCAP Harold Arlen Award, The New York Musical Festival's Outstanding Lyrics Award, and the Edgerton New Play Award. Matt lives in Los Angeles with his wife and two daughters. Learn more at mattschatz.com.

This project was made possible, in part, by generous support from the Osage Arts Community.

Osage Arts Community provides temporary time, space and support for the creation of new artistic works in a retreat format, serving creative people of all kinds — visual artists, composers, poets, fiction and nonfiction writers. Located on a 152-acre farm in an isolated rural mountainside setting in Central Missouri and bordered by ¾ of a mile of the Gasconade River, OAC provides residencies to those working alone, as well as welcoming collaborative teams, offering living space and workspace in a country environment to emerging and mid-career artists. For more information, visit us at www.osageac.org

Osage Arts Community